THE DNA GAVE IT AWAY!

TEENS SOLVE CRIME

Yvonne Morrison

children's press®

An imprint of Scholastic Inc.

NEW YORK • TORONTO • LONDON • AUCKLAND • SYDNEY
MEXICO CITY • NEW DELHI • HONG KONG
DANBURY, CONNECTICUT

Library of Congress Cataloging-in-Publication Data

Morrison, Yvonne, 1972-
The DNA gave it away! : teens solve crime / by Yvonne Morrison.
p. cm. -- (Shockwave)
Includes index.

ISBN-10: 0-531-17581-2 (lib. bdg.)
ISBN-13: 978-0-531-17581-1 (lib. bdg.)
ISBN-10: 0-531-18842-6 (pbk.)
ISBN-13: 978-0-531-18842-2 (pbk.)

1. Criminal investigation--Juvenile literature. 2. Forensic
sciences--Juvenile literature. 3. DNA fingerprinting--Juvenile
literature. I. Title. II. Series.

HV8073.8.M67 2008
363.25'62--dc22
2007010063
323.44--dc22
2007010061

Published in 2008 by Children's Press, an imprint of Scholastic Inc.,
557 Broadway, New York, New York 10012
www.scholastic.com

08 09 10 11 12 13 14 15 16 17
10 9 8 7 6 5 4 3 2

Printed in China through Colorcraft Ltd., Hong Kong

Author: Yvonne Morrison
Editor: Janine Scott
Designer: Carol Hsu
Photo Researcher: Jamshed Mistry

Photographs by: aapimage.com/EPA (technician holding X-ray, p. 17); **David Flynn**
(cotton and synthetic fibers, p. 18); **Getty Images** (pp. 6–7); **Jennifer and Brian Lupton**
(children, pp. 30–31); **Photolibrary** (p. 5; p. 9; p. 11; p. 13; p. 15; scientist, p. 19;
p. 20; pp. 21–22; check, p. 22; cell phone, p. 23; crime scene, p. 25; pp. 26–29;
DNA printout, pp. 30–31); **Tranz/Corbis** (police dog, p. 10; diatoms, p. 19; computer,
p. 23; court scene, p. 25)

The publisher would like to thank David Flynn of Victoria University of Wellington,
New Zealand, for providing the photographs of fibers on page 18.

All other photographs and illustrations © Weldon Owen Education Inc.

CONTENTS

HIGH-POWERED WORDS	4
GET ON THE WAVELENGTH	6
The Crime Scene	8
Collecting Clues	10
Sticky Fingers	12
Making Tracks	14
Teeth Tell Tales	16
Under the Microscope	18
The DNA Gave It Away	20
Document Clues	22
Whodunit?	24
Forensic Science Careers	26
Dead Giveaways	28
AFTERSHOCKS	30
GLOSSARY	32
INDEX	32

EVIDENCE FILE

crime scene the place where a crime has been committed

DNA the molecules in every cell of an organism that carry the genetic code, which determines characteristics of that organism, such as eye color

DNA profile the analysis of DNA using samples, such as hair and blood, to identify people

evidence information that may link a person to a crime

forensic relating to using scientific methods, such as fingerprinting, to solve a crime

suspect a person who is believed to be responsible for a crime or an accident

victim a person who is injured or killed as a result of a crime or an accident

For easy reference, see Wordmark on back flap.
For additional vocabulary, see Glossary on page 32.

DNA is an acronym. Acronyms are words or groups of letters that are used as a short form. You might be familiar with other acronyms, such as NASA, UNICEF, and LASER. DNA is short for deoxyribonucleic (*dee OKS ih rye bo noo clay ik*) acid. No wonder we use an acronym!

A **forensic** scientist uses a special lamp and glasses to find fingerprints.

Many crimes are solved with the help of witnesses, or even the **victims** themselves. However, when there are no witnesses and the victim is unable to help, then **DNA** and other clues can help solve a crime.

Along with the police, **forensic** scientists are the first to arrive at a **crime scene**. They carefully search the area for clues, such as a knife. Then they photograph and collect the clues, bag them, and analyze them back at the **laboratory**.

Forensic scientists use many methods to find the person who committed a crime. They can use the same methods to eliminate **suspects**. They may study the handwriting left on a note. They may analyze people's computers and cell phones. They can use footprints and even bite marks to link someone to a crime. Today, it is harder than ever to commit a crime and get away with it.

Forensic scientists can tell how long ago a person died by studying the body.

Moment of death
A person's heart stops beating.

Within minutes
A thin film forms over the eyes. The eyeballs go soft.

Before 3 hours
Some muscles begin to stiffen. This is called **rigor mortis**.

After 3 hours
Open eyes turn cloudy.

After 6–12 hours
Rigor mortis takes over the whole body. Muscles may stay stiff for as long as 12 hours.

After 12–24 hours
Rigor mortis disappears.

After 48 hours
The skin may turn greenish, due to bacterial action.

After 4–7 days
The skin may appear marbled.

THE CRIME SCENE

For two weeks, Eduardo and some other students would be studying forensic science for one hour a day. The subject fascinated Eduardo. He liked solving mysteries.

Ms. Scott, the chemistry teacher, came into the hallway. "Come in," she said, "but don't touch anything. A crime has been committed in this lab. Someone has stolen a valuable diamond!"

Ms. Scott led the students to the corner of the lab, which was roped off with bright-yellow tape. She handed out vinyl gloves and lab coats, and asked the students to put them on. "Welcome to the scene of the crime," she said, winking.

Then she handed the students different equipment and instructions. "Here are our three suspects," said Ms. Scott, pointing to photos on the whiteboard. "They are not real criminals. We are only pretending. You have two weeks to solve the crime and catch the thief!"

Suspect A   Suspect B   Suspect C

CRIME SCENE   CRIME SCENE   CRIME SCE

When forensic scientists arrive at the crime scene, they follow special procedures to make sure all the **evidence** is collected properly. They must be careful not to **contaminate** the scene. They wear protective suits with hoods, a face mask, gloves, and special overshoes.

The left-hand page is written as a story, and the right-hand page has real information. That makes the book more interesting, and it makes the subject easier to understand.

Forensic scientists use many tools to collect clues. At the crime scene, numbered markers are used to indicate where each piece of evidence is found.

COLLECTING CLUES

Eduardo was given a camera. He started taking close-up photos of absolutely everything at the scene. He was careful not to disturb any evidence. After Eduardo had recorded each piece of evidence, Latisha and Joel picked it up with tweezers. They put it in a plastic bag. Juliana took the bag and labeled it with a marker.

All the students were involved in the investigation. Craig and Theo measured a footprint on the floor. Hannah and Kim-Lee dusted surfaces with powder to find fingerprints. Danika and Alicia put on their gloves. They sorted through the classroom trash can.

At the end of the lesson, Ms. Scott took the camera and the evidence. She locked them in a drawer. She didn't want them **tampered** with.

"See you tomorrow," she said. "Remember to bring your notebooks. Beginning tomorrow, everyone will be keeping a crime-scene journal."

FORENSIC FACT

Forensic scientists can capture smells at a crime scene. The chemicals in the smell stick to a scent pad, which is then freeze-dried for later use. Trained dogs are used to match a crime-scene smell to a suspect.

CRIME CLUES

Forensic scientists work together with the police to collect evidence. It is important that the crime scene be protected so that no one can remove clues. The crime scene is sealed off with crime-scene tape. A police officer stands guard.

Forensic scientists search for clues at a crime scene. A police photographer takes pictures of all the evidence.

The evidence is collected with tweezers. Sometimes fibers and hairs are collected with a suction-tube device.

The evidence is bagged and labeled. It is analyzed in a laboratory. Then it is kept in police storage.

Crime-scene investigators are thorough. They:

- make sure the scene is protected
- search carefully for clues
- photograph as much as possible
- bag and label evidence

STICKY FINGERS

Today, we looked at the fingerprints that Hannah and Kim-Lee collected. There were five clear prints and four partial prints. We used a magnifying glass to look at the fingerprint patterns. One of the prints matched Suspect B's prints. The other prints didn't match Suspect A or Suspect C's prints. Alicia suggested we look at Ms. Scott's prints. They matched! Ms. Scott is in the lab all the time, so she leaves fingerprints everywhere. I guess that **innocent** people leave evidence too!

| Evidence fingerprint | Suspect B's fingerprint | Ms. Scott's fingerprint |

Ridges on the finger form patterns. The three main patterns are whorls, loops, and arches. No two people have exactly the same patterns.

Forensic File

| Whorl | Loop | Arch |

Three Kinds of Fingerprints to Look For

- Plastic prints: pressed into a soft surface, such as soap

- Latent prints: left behind by oils from the skin

- Patent prints: made with something visible, such as ink

Fingerprints left on **nonporous** surfaces, such as china, glass, and plastic, can be dusted with powder and lifted with transparent tape.

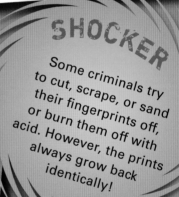

Some criminals try to cut, scrape, or sand their fingerprints off, or burn them off with acid. However, the prints always grow back identically!

Magnetic powders can be used on some **porous** surfaces. Iron filings in the powder stick to sweat. The unstuck filings are lifted off with a magnet to reveal the prints.

Forensic File

13

MAKING TRACKS

Today, Ms. Scott showed us some shoes that she had collected from the suspects. We looked at my photo of a footprint that was found on the lab floor. Theo and Craig told us how long and how wide it was. We compared it with the suspects' shoes. It matched Suspect A's shoe.

Two Kinds of Footprints to Look For

- Footwear mark: a footprint left on a hard surface

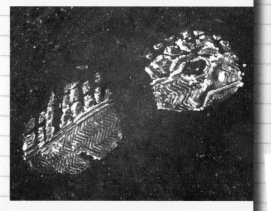

- Depressed mark: a footprint left in a soft surface

Many of the compound words that appear on these pages, such as *footprints*, *footwear*, and *fingerprints*, involve body parts. There are also compound words that begin with other body parts, such as *headache*, *kneecap*, *eyeball*, and *brainwave*.

Fingerprints are not the only marks that criminals leave behind. Bare feet, lips, and even ears leave telltale marks. Tread marks from car or bicycle tires and the soles of shoes can also link a suspect to a crime.

Many people own the same brand of tires or shoes. However, tires and shoes can wear out differently. Forensic scientists study worn patches and defects on a shoe. If a worn left heel on a shoe matches a print with a worn left heel, then it is proof that it belongs to the same person.

Scientists can't pick up a patch of mud that has a tire or shoe print in it. Instead, they pour plaster into the print and let it harden. The plaster cast is a copy of the tire or shoe sole that made the print. Scientists can then match it to a suspect's car or shoe.

Because of the heading, and what I have already read on the previous pages, I am pretty sure these pages will tell me about how teeth are used as evidence.

Danika and Alicia found a cheese sandwich in the trash can. It had a bite out of it. The shape of the bite was very clear. Ms. Scott gave us photos of the suspects' teeth. The teeth of Suspect A and Suspect B matched quite well, but Suspect C's front teeth were crooked.

Evidence

Sandwich: Bite Mark
Found: Trash Can

Forensic File

No two people have the same bite pattern. People may have gaps between teeth, crooked teeth, and teeth with braces. If a criminal has bitten something at a crime scene, scientists can match the bite mark to the criminal's teeth.

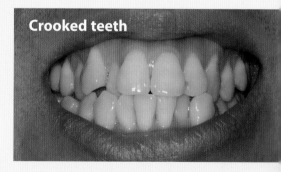

Crooked teeth

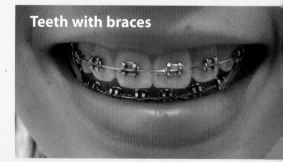

Teeth with braces

Sometimes when a skeleton is found, police have a hard time working out who the person was. Teeth can help forensic dentists identify dead bodies. Forensic dentists can take X-rays of the skull. If they think they know whose body it is, they can compare the X-rays with that person's dental records.

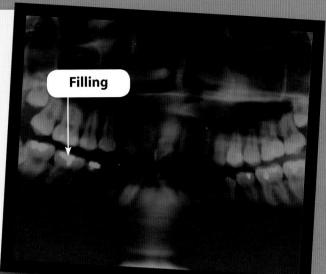

Filling

FORENSIC FACT

In 1954, a bite mark in a piece of cheese landed a robber in jail! Police found the cheese when they went to investigate a robbery at a grocery store in Texas. It was the first bite-mark case in the United States.

UNDER THE MICROSCOPE

Fibers found on a lab bench.

Today, we looked at some yellow clothing fibers that were found snagged on a lab bench. Suspect A was wearing a red cotton shirt. Suspect B had a yellow cotton shirt. Suspect C was wearing a yellow **synthetic** sweater. When we looked under a microscope, we could see that cotton and synthetic fibers were very different. The evidence was definitely yellow cotton fibers.

Fiber Facts

Natural fibers come from plants and animals. Synthetic fibers are made from chemicals. Different fibers have different structures.

Cotton fibers

Synthetic fibers

Natural Fibers

Sheep

Wool

Flax

Linen

Cotton plant

Cotton

Scientists study fibers, soil, seeds, and pollen under microscopes. Sometimes a particular kind of evidence is found only in a specific area. For example, soil found on a suspect's shoe could match soil samples from the scene of the crime.

Diatoms

Diatoms are tiny plants found in both freshwater and salt water. The lungs of a person who has drowned will contain many diatoms. Scientists can check for diatoms using a high-powered microscope.

19

THE DNA GAVE IT AWAY

We talked about hair and blood today. Some short, brown hairs and a few long, black ones were found on the bench. Suspect B has short, brown hair. Suspect A has long, black hair, but so does Ms. Scott. How can we tell whether the black hair came from Ms. Scott or Suspect A? We need to do DNA testing. Unfortunately, we can't do that at our school.

It's the same with the blood. We found some drops of blood on some broken glass. Real scientists would be able to test the DNA in the blood to find out whose it is.

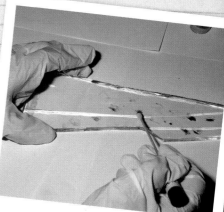

Drops of blood found on some broken glass.

FORENSIC FACT

Your DNA is what makes you look like you. Every living thing, including every human being, is made up of trillion of tiny packets called cells. Every cell contains DNA, or deoxyribonucleic acid. DNA is a long **molecule** made up of chemicals linked together in a pattern that forms a code. No two people have the same code, except for identical twins.

DNA profiling is a method used to identify someone's DNA. A chemical is used to cut the DNA molecules into pieces. The chemical will create different-sized pieces for each person's sample, because each person has a unique DNA molecule. A pattern of dark bands like a bar code is formed when the pieces of DNA are put into a special gel.

DNA

What It Is	How Obtained	Method for Profiling
code inside a cell, made up of a long molecule	swabs of blood or other body fluids or tissues	pieces arranged in special gel; these form a unique pattern

SHOCKER

A cat's DNA helped solve a murder! A victim's blood-stained jacket was covered with white cat fur. The victim's ex-husband had a white cat. Experts matched the fur to his cat.

Forensic scientists take **swabs** of blood and other body fluids. The swabs are stored in sealed containers. They are tested at the lab.

POLICE EVIDENCE BAG

DOCUMENT CLUES

Ms. Scott received a letter today. It was handwritten.

> If you want to get the diamond back, put one million dollars in the trash can outside the school tonight!

We studied the note. We looked at the way the letters were written. The t's were crossed down low. The g's had big loops. The m's and n's were wide and flat. The i's had no dots above them. We looked at samples of the suspects' writing. Suspect B was the closest, but the loops in the g's were narrower. Perhaps he had tried to disguise his handwriting.

Using **ultraviolet (UV) light**, experts proved that the 6 and *six* on this British check were changed to *60* and *sixty*.

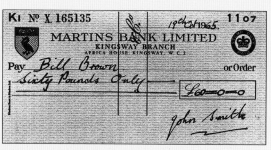

Under normal light

Under UV light

Did You Know?

Document examiners are experts at studying handwriting. They can compare the way people form their letters. When people write normally, the letters flow. When they try to disguise their writing, it stops and starts and looks clumsy. Some criminals **forge** handwriting. Experts can tell the difference.

Cell phones can hold a suspect's personal information. Police can trace incoming and outgoing phone numbers. The location of the phone at the time of these phone calls can also be traced.

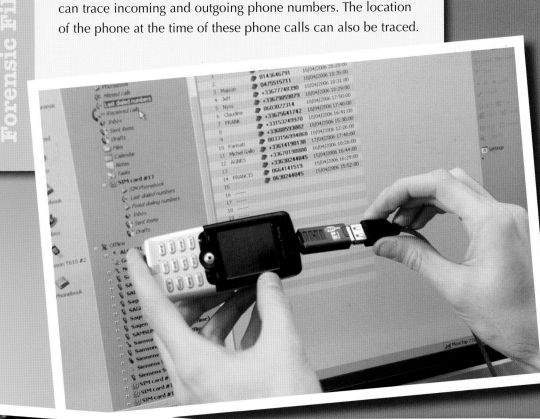

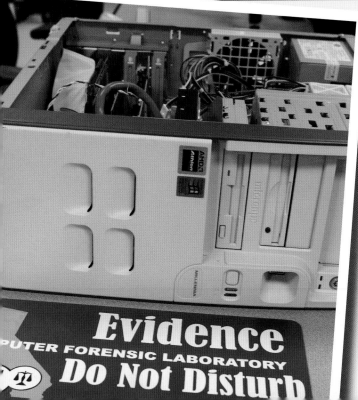

Computers store valuable evidence. Documents can be retrieved even after they have been deleted. Computer printers make different marks and have different inks. E-mail can be traced to find out who a suspect has been communicating with.

Evidence

PUTER FORENSIC LABORATORY

Do Not Disturb

WHODUNIT?

Today, we reviewed the evidence. We read our journals out loud and said who we thought had done it. I said Suspect B. His fingerprint was at the scene, and so was his hair. He was wearing clothing that matched the fibers. He could have bitten the cheese sandwich. His writing almost matched the note. Juliana argued that it could have been Suspect A. Her shoeprint was at the scene, and the black hair and the sandwich might have been hers.

In the end, we made a decision. We would suggest that the police arrest Suspect B. Maybe Suspect A was his **accomplice**, but there wasn't enough evidence to arrest her.

That's interesting. The heading is a question. It's as if the author is talking directly to me! I don't think she wants an answer. I think she just wants me to think about the question as I read these pages.

Forensic File

Computers can be used to create a 3-D reconstruction of a crime scene. This is useful in the event that the crime scene no longer exists.

AT COURT

SHOCKER

Brainwave fingerprinting is the newest technique. A suspect watches images from the crime scene. If the memory is already in the suspect's brain, there will be a different brainwave response. The suspect's mind is being read!

Forensic scientists study the evidence. They send their reports to the police.

⬇

The police arrest and charge a suspect with a crime if there is enough evidence.

⬇

The lawyers read the scientists' reports to see what the evidence is.

⬇

A trial takes place in a court of law.

⬇

The **prosecution** lawyer will try to show that the evidence proves that the accused is guilty.

⬇

The **defense** lawyer will try to show that there might be another explanation.

⬇

Scientists may be called to court to discuss the forensic evidence.

⬇

A jury decides if the accused is guilty.

Forensic File

25

FORENSIC SCIENCE
CAREERS

We were right! Ms. Scott told us that Suspect B confessed to the crime. Suspect A was innocent. She had just come into the lab to borrow some equipment.

Of course, this wasn't a real crime. Ms. Scott doesn't keep diamonds in her lab! But it taught me a lot about forensic science. Now I know what I want to do when I finish school!

Suspect B

GUILTY

CASE CLOSED

Forensic scientists often specialize. A ballistics expert knows all about guns and bullets. When a gun fires a bullet, grooves in the metal lining of the gun barrel leave marks on the bullet. Scientists can use them to match the bullet to the gun.

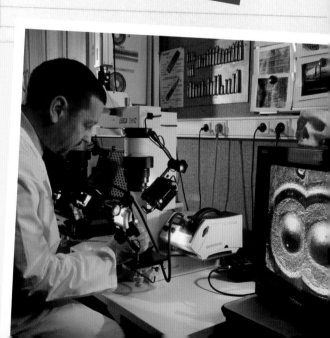

Traffic-accident investigators can work out how vehicles have collided. They measure skid marks and collect evidence, such as broken headlights and paint samples.

SHOCKER

Flies and other insects can help a forensic scientist tell how long a person has been dead. The insects lay their eggs at different times. They also feed on different tissues!

Forensic **entomologists** study insects. Different insects live in different parts of the world. Insects found in evidence can show where the evidence came from.

DEAD GIVEAWAYS

When someone dies unexpectedly, a **pathologist** has to investigate. The pathologist carries out a **postmortem**, or autopsy, which is a study of the dead body. First the body is X-rayed, weighed, and measured. The pathologist looks all over the outside of the body for any strange marks, such as burns, bruises, cuts, or scrapes. The body is then cut open and the organs are examined. The contents of the stomach can show what the person ate for his or her last meal, and when. The pathologist also takes the temperature of the body to find out when the person died.

All these procedures can tell a pathologist whether the person died from natural or accidental causes, or was murdered. Sometimes police do not know who the dead person was. The pathologist can try to get clues from the body.

The term *postmortem* comes from the Latin words *post*, meaning "after," and *mortem*, meaning "death." So *postmortem* means "after death." The word meaning "before death" is *antemortem*.

Forensic File

Sometimes people who witness a crime remember some particular feature about a person, such as a scar or a tattoo. These external marks can help to identify a suspect.

Scar

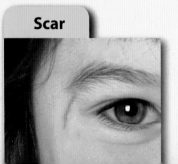

Tattoo

Even a skeleton contains much information about a person. By measuring the length and shape of the bones, scientists can tell the person's height, age, race, and gender.

SHOCKER

If a body is too damaged to get a fingerprint, the finger is cut off and its skin turned inside out to get a print from the inside!

Some scientists are experts at using a human skull to reconstruct a face. A computer program adds layers of facial muscles and skin to a 3-D image of the skull. It builds up a likeness of a victim.

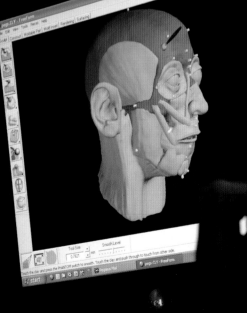

In many places, all criminals convicted of a violent crime have their DNA recorded and stored in a computer file. If the criminal ever commits another crime and leaves DNA behind, the computer will match it. Other places record the DNA of every convicted criminal, even if the crime wasn't serious. Some DNA **databases** contain DNA records not only of criminals, but also of people

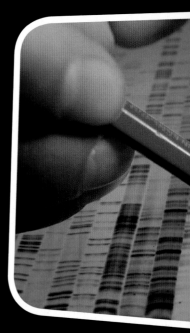

WHAT DO YOU THINK?

Should everyone in the world have their DNA stored on file?

PRO

It's a good idea to store DNA records. People who commit crimes and leave DNA behind are caught more easily. If people don't commit crimes, they have nothing to worry about. The police won't be interested in them.

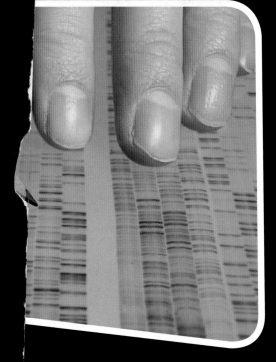

who have been arrested and then found not guilty of a crime.

Some people think that everyone should have their DNA recorded at a certain age. This would mean that many more criminals would be caught. Dead bodies would also be easier to identify. Some people think this is private information that should never be viewed by others.

CON

I don't want my DNA to be on file. It shows that the police don't trust me. What if someone tampers with the computer file? What if someone looks at my DNA file and finds out something about my health? I don't want other people knowing private things about me!

Go to **www.genetics.gsk. com/kids/index_kids.htm** to learn more about DNA.

accomplice a person who helps another person commit a crime

contaminate to make dirty or unfit for use

database a structured set of information stored in a computer

defense arguing in favor of the accused, or defendant, in a court trial

entomologist a scientist who studies insects

forge to make illegal copies of paintings, money, or other items

innocent not guilty of a crime or an offense

laboratory a room or building containing the equipment used for scientific experiments

molecule the smallest part of a substance that has all the chemical properties of that substance

nonporous lacking openings that would allow a liquid or a gas to pass through

pathologist a medical doctor who specializes in studying human tissue to find the cause of disease or death

porous full of tiny holes that let liquid or gas pass through

postmortem an examination of a dead body to determine the cause of death

prosecution arguing in a court trial that the accused, or defendant, is guilty of the crime

rigor mortis the stiffening of joints and muscles a few hours after death

swab a sample of fluid taken with an absorbent pad

synthetic manufactured or artificial; not found in nature

tamper to handle or interfere with something so that it becomes damaged or broken

ultraviolet light energy rays with a shorter wavelength than visible light

ballistics 26
blood 20–21
brainwave fingerprinting 25
cell phones 7, 23
computers 7, 23–24, 29–31
diatoms 19
dogs 10
fibers 11, 18–19, 24
fingerprints 5, 10, 12–15, 24, 29
footprints 7, 10, 14–15, 24
hair 11, 20, 24
handwriting 7, 22, 24
insects 27
photography 6, 8, 10–11, 14, 16
plaster casts 15
police 6, 11, 17, 23–25, 28, 30–31
skeletons 17, 29
smells 10
teeth 16–17
tools 9
traffic-accident investigators 27
tread marks 15
trials 25
witnesses 6, 28